MR. FLEMING'S

NEW MEXICO FORAGING GUIDE
OF
WILD EDIBLE PLANTS AND MUSHROOMS

Foraging New Mexico :
What, Where & How to Forage
along with Colored Interior, Photos & Recipes

Stephen Fleming

© Copyright 2022 - All rights reserved.

The content contained within this book may not be reproduced, duplicated or transmitted without direct written permission from the author or the publisher.

Under no circumstances will any blame or legal responsibility be held against the publisher, or author, for any damages, reparation, or monetary loss due to the information contained within this book, either directly or indirectly.

Legal Notice:
This book is copyright protected. It is only for personal use. You cannot amend, distribute, sell, use, quote, or paraphrase any part, or the content within this book, without the author or publisher's consent.

Disclaimer Notice:
Please note the information contained within this document is for educational and entertainment purposes only. All effort has been executed to present accurate, up-to-date, reliable, complete information. No warranties of any kind are declared or implied. Readers acknowledge that the author is not engaged in the rendering of legal, financial, medical or professional advice. The content within this book has been derived from various sources. Please consult a licensed professional before attempting any techniques outlined in this book.

By reading this document, the reader agrees that under no circumstances is the author responsible for any losses, direct or indirect, that are incurred as a result of the use of the information contained within this document, including, but not limited to, errors, omissions, or inaccuracies.

Disclaimer

- Each individual is solely responsible for doing their own research and due diligence and comparing with multiple sources before consuming any fungi or wild plant.

- The book's objective is simply to provide information; it is not intended to replace diagnosis and treatment, tasks that pertain to a doctor.

- The contents of this book are for informational purposes and are not intended to offer personal medical advice.

- You should seek the advice of your physician or another qualified health provider regarding a medical condition. Never disregard professional medical advice or delay seeking it because of something you have read in this book. The book does not recommend or endorse any products.

- Any book, video, or other means of learning can't replace learning physically from an expert. These forms of information are only additional guidance to be used along with a practical demonstration and training.

- Always check the legal status of the plant you intend to forage and use.

- This is just a reference book and is in no way responsible for any health-related issue caused by eating wild plants or fungi. Do your due diligence before consuming any wild food.

Table of Contents

Introduction

Chapter 1: Foraging in New Mexico: What's Legal and Not.

Chapter 2: Ethical Foraging

Chapter 3: Why Forage-Benefits

Chapter 4: Foraging in New Mexico: Where to Forage

Chapter 5: What to Forage: Meet Wild Edible plants & Mushrooms of New Mexico

Chapter 6: Storing Foraged Goods

Chapter 7: Let's Cook: 10 Edible Wild Plant Recipes

Chapter 8: Conclusion

Appendix - Foraging Tips, Foraging Classes & Tours, Mushroom Identification Logbook Pages

Introduction

Foraging is the age-old practice of searching for and gathering wild foods. It is the primary way in which our ancestors survived in the past before they discovered agricultural practices. If you are reading this book, you may already have some experience foraging or just be learning about it now. This guide focuses on foraging in the southwest, specifically in New Mexico. Foragers will find so many new wild foods they have never tried before while walking through the bio-diverse habitats in this region.

The modern lifestyle is very different from how our ancestors lived. There were no grocery stores and processed foods, and there was no need to spend much money on food. If you want to change your current lifestyle and diet for the better, foraging might be a real help. You will be surprised by how many different edible foods grow outside in the wild. You can still buy your usual groceries but imagine how much you would save if you could learn how to forage for free food. There is an abundance of delicious plants and fungi that you will find around New Mexico.

As you read through the book, you will learn a lot about how foraging should be practiced ethically and where you can find edible wild foods around this area. You will also learn how to preserve extra harvests and store food for the winter. Foraged food is healthier than all the processed foods or the products you buy in stores since there are no pesticides or harmful additives involved.

These are all plant foods that nature provides you with at no cost or effort. It would be best if you learned what to look for and how to correctly identify the plants. Safely identifying wild plants is crucial since many plants may be toxic but look similar. You also have to know which parts are safe for consumption and which aren't. For instance, the leaves and stems on some plants may be safe to eat, but the berries might be toxic.

Joshua tree in the desert in New Mexico with the blue sky

This is why knowledge is key for safe foraging practices. Use the right plant guides and look for distinct characteristics that help you correctly identify wild plants or fungi. Over time, you will learn enough to rely on yourself when you set out foraging. However, for now, you can use this book and other foraging guides to help you find delicious wild foods in the wilds of New Mexico.

So, start reading and venture into the wild!

Bisti/De-Na-Zin Wilderness of Northern New Mexico
Photo by John Fowler on Unsplash

Foraged Products

1. Foraging in New Mexico: What's Legal and What's Not

New Mexico has abundant wild edible plants, but you need to know where you can legally forage. The laws and regulations for every part of the country may differ regarding foraging, and you need to familiarize yourself with the laws to avoid any trouble.

Paying attention to the legalities is an important part of ethical foraging. You may be free to forage in some places, need permission in certain areas, or be completely forbidden from foraging in some places as well. Since there is a lot of interest in foraging, it can affect the wild plant ecosystems if laws are not enforced properly.

Always look into the specific laws applicable in your area. Some places, like California, completely prohibit foraging in almost any state-owned land, while others, like Hawaii, are much more lenient. New Mexico has had a history of foraging with all its Native American and Hispanic history. However, some laws determine where what and how much you can harvest. You have to ensure that you follow these.

Gathering wild edibles growing on the roadsides or sidewalks is generally okay. However, you should only pick small amounts and never the whole plant. Pick the leaves or fruit you might see but don't pull out the roots. While foraging for wild mushrooms for personal use, the limit is three types and one gallon only per type of mushroom. Anything more than that will require a permit or cost you a fine.

The state laws only allow you to pick and transport an amount for personal consumption.

If you venture into any area that falls under a National Forest, you should only forage after contacting the Forest Service office of that locality. They will tell you the harvesting regulations applicable to that region. These may also vary according to season. Always follow the applicable laws to avoid any fines or possible jail time.

It is easier to forage from private properties simply by asking permission from the landowners. They have rights over the plants growing on their properties, and you don't have to worry about what laws are applicable there.

Tips for Beginner Forager

Know poisonous species	Don't disturb nature with your activity	Assist an expert on foraging walks first
Focus on area with abundant weeds	Study about flora & fauna of the area beforehand	Check the local rules before venturing

If you ask nicely, most neighbors will allow you to harvest wild food from their land. You can also talk and let them know that you will practice ethical foraging and not damage the plants or anything on their property.

Offer some wild foods or anything else from your property in exchange if you can. You can also offer to de-weed their lawn if you identify edible weeds. It's a win-win situation for everyone. This is one of the simplest ways to forage from some places without any legal hassle.

Safety Measures

Since foraging is only enjoyable when it's risk-free, there are a few guidelines to comply with:

- Only consume something if you're one hundred percent certain of its identity.

- Always obtain approval before collecting from another person's land. Some national and state parks enable limited quantities of foraging of certain plants.

- Stay out of hectic roads or parking lots. The plants there may contain pollutants.

- Don't forage there if you suspect an area has been splashed with insecticides or herbicides.

- Start with a small amount of foraged food. This way, if you have an allergy, it will be manageable.

Mushroom Foraging in New Mexico- Tips

- Go mushroom hunting with a person who has New Mexico regional experience.

- Sign up with a local club like the New Mexico Mycological Society.

- Carry a New Mexico mushroom identification book and a log book.

- If you do not like the smell of a mushroom, leave it, even if someone informs you it's edible.

- Do not put mushrooms you accumulate in plastic bags; they will certainly sweat. Use cloth and wax paper. Put various types of mushrooms in different packets/bags.

Cacti tree cholla cylindropuntia imbricata in New Mexico

About New Mexico

- New Mexico includes almost 78 million acres of land mass.

- More than 90 percent of which is in native vegetation.

- There are more than 3,000 species of plants in New Mexico.

- New Mexico has many vast wilderness areas developed as state and local parks within the national forests.

- New Mexico has numerous dangerous plants. These plants create various signs, symptoms, and ailment extents.

- Very hazardous/poisonous plants consist of but are not limited to the following: foxglove, oleander, jimson weed, and exterior mushrooms.

- The state includes four regions:
  - The Great Plains
  - The Colorado Plateau
  - The Rocky Mountains
  - The Basin and Range area.

- New Mexico has a few of the flattest land and a few of the most challenging mountains in the nation. As a result, some parts of the state are rich in ache forests, meadows, and fish-laden hill streams, while others lack water bodies and cacti battles to endure.

2. Ethical Foraging

Many people surpass this foraging aspect, but we should not be one of them. Ethical foraging is a way of life that you should instill within yourself. It is not enough to pick a pair of scissors and snip whatever wild foods you find into your basket. Foraging is all about responsibility and reciprocity. It is about respecting what came before and what will come after us.

Principles of Ethical Foraging

Practice Legal Foraging

Laws and regulations are in place to help prevent overexploitation of the environment for one. Without these, people would be harvesting everything they could find and damaging the local ecosystems. Laws are in place to protect plants that may be receding in number and might soon be extinct.

Foraging Mushroom

You have to check the laws and regulations of the place you intend to forage around. You can get permits where it is required. Also, please get permission from any landowner before plucking anything off their land. Many people walk into properties without knowing that it is private. You may unknowingly attract trouble.

The best way to avoid this is to ask for permission wherever possible. If you want to pluck fruits from your neighbor's tree, you could always offer something in exchange or assure them that you will only take a few.

Foraging basket

Take Only As Much As You Need

This is one of the most important aspects of ethical foraging. It might be tempting to pluck all the tree's berries or pull out the entire plant because it is edible.However, you probably don't need that much wild food, and a lot of it might go to waste. Another reason not to do this is that you would be causing undue stress on the plant and the micro-ecosystem.

This would prevent the plant from bearing fruit again and would also not leave enough food for the wildlife around. Instead, harvest from abundant plants and leave the solitary ones alone. Take only as much as you need and harvest more from plants that grow faster.

Triple-Check the Identification of a Plant Before Harvesting

Proper identification of the plant is important for several reasons. One main reason is that you can prevent mishaps and eat only safe wild edibles.

Another is that you can then leave the other plants alone in their natural surroundings. There is no point in picking a lot of plant parts only to throw them away later. If you don't check the plant properly, you might consume a toxic lookalike and fall sick.

Harvest From the Right Areas

Avoid harvesting from places where the plants are likely to be exposed to contaminants. For instance, plants that grow near agricultural fields will likely have absorbed the pesticides and other chemicals used there.

Plants growing near busy roadsides also absorb many pollutants from cars. It is best to leave such areas alone and not consume the poisonous plants.

These would do more harm than good for your body. Also, avoid over-harvesting from the same spots. Go a little deeper instead of plucking from the same plants from which others have been picking wild food. This will give the plants a chance to replenish and regrow. You can always come back later.

Leave Things as They Were or Better

Carry a little bag or basket to pick up any trash. Don't trample over all the wild plants carelessly, and don't pluck off whole plants. Leave an as little trace of your being there as possible. This will help protect the micro-ecosystem and ensure you can return to harvest safely from there again. Don't disturb any nests or chop off plants roughly.

Use the Right Tools

This is one way of protecting and respecting nature. The right tools will help you harvest from plants appropriately. This will help them regrow again and prevent you from taking more than you need. The right tools will also help you safely carry the wild foods home.

If you keep these ethical practices in mind, foraging will always be a rewarding experience.

Tools

3. The Benefits Of Foraging

If you are new to foraging, you may still wonder if you should or shouldn't delve into this practice. The answer is affirmative because of all the benefits of foraging. There are no cons to being a forager, and so many ways it will improve the overall quality of your life. Here are some reasons to convince you to become a forager:

Benefits

Better Physical Health

Walking around in the wild or just about anywhere to look for wild foods will help improve your physical health. You will get a lot of steps in, enhancing your cardiac health while also helping you lose excess weight.

You can even explore more challenging terrain and go hiking, which will help you burn more calories and strengthen your muscles.

The sedentary modern-day lifestyle allows most people to spend entire days without taking more than a few steps around. As a forager, you will develop the habit of becoming a lot more active and thus benefit your physical health in the long term.

Better Mental Health

While many focus on physical health, mental health often takes the backseat. With foraging, you improve your mental health just as much as your physical health.

As you are more active you become, you release good hormones like dopamine that make you feel better. You also step out into the sun more often, and vitamin D is the best way to improve your mood.

Your mind becomes calmer as you immerse yourself in your surroundings while foraging. Spending more time in greenery is scientifically proven to improve mental health. So the more you walk around looking for wild food, the better you will feel.

Reduce Expenses

With inflation, prices of food have been increasing every single year. This means your grocery bills seem to rise all the time. As a forager, you will be able to make the best of all the free wild foods growing around you.

You can find so many delicious edibles in the wild that would otherwise cost you a lot at a store.

You will also discover new foods you might not have been familiar with. Nature provides you with free food for nothing in return. All you have to do is walk out and learn a little about what is edible or inedible.

Connect With Nature

Foraging allows you to reconnect with nature. While our ancestors were much more in tune with the land, plants, and overall environment, our generation is very detached.

This has allowed people to treat the planet with little care and caused issues like global warming. As a forager, you start noticing everything from the weather to how the soil feels. You reestablish the connection that humans are supposed to have with nature. This will benefit you as well as future generations. As an ethical forager, you will learn how to respect nature again.

Eat Healthier

Wild foods grow all on their own. There are no fertilizers, pesticides, insecticides, etc. that are used. When you buy food from grocery stores, your body indirectly absorbs all these harmful contaminants.

With foraging, you get access to free organic food that is nutritious and devoid of such contaminants. While organic food would cost you a lot at the store, it costs nothing to a forager. Your body gets access to natural foods that only benefit it.

Connect With Like-Minded People

Foragers can connect with other foragers in their community or online.

These people will share many of your values and enrich your life. You get to participate in foraging walks and other community events with them. Establishing such connections through foraging will enrich your life with the right people.

With all these benefits in mind, you would have no reason to second-guess the start of your foraging journey.

Foraging Produce

Brush, Magnifying Glass & Field Guide

So, as you might have understood now, a lot of learning is involved. This journey becomes easier if you are aware of all the different benefits it offers.

Also, for those looking for a new hobby for physical and mental well-being, Foraging is! Foraging is incredibly enjoyable and relaxing. If you want a new hobby, start spending more time outdoors by becoming a forager.

4. Foraging in New Mexico: Where to Forage?

Wild edible plants grow all around you, but it can help many of you know exactly where to look. This chapter will help you learn about some of the best spots to go foraging in New Mexico.

New Mexicans have been foraging for hundreds of years. There are all kinds of delicious wild plants that you will discover when you go foraging in these areas.

(1) Northern and Central Mountains

The Northern and Central Mountains of New Mexico include Sangre de Cristo, Sandia, Manzano, and Jemez.

There are numerous microclimates around these mountains, and you can discover a lot of different wild plants growing at different times throughout the year.

In general, you can start foraging there around April at higher elevations and by March in places at lower elevations. Dandelions grow prolifically in these areas near Taos or Santa Fe. This weed is rich in vitamin C, iron, and minerals.

Dandelions

Regions of New Mexico

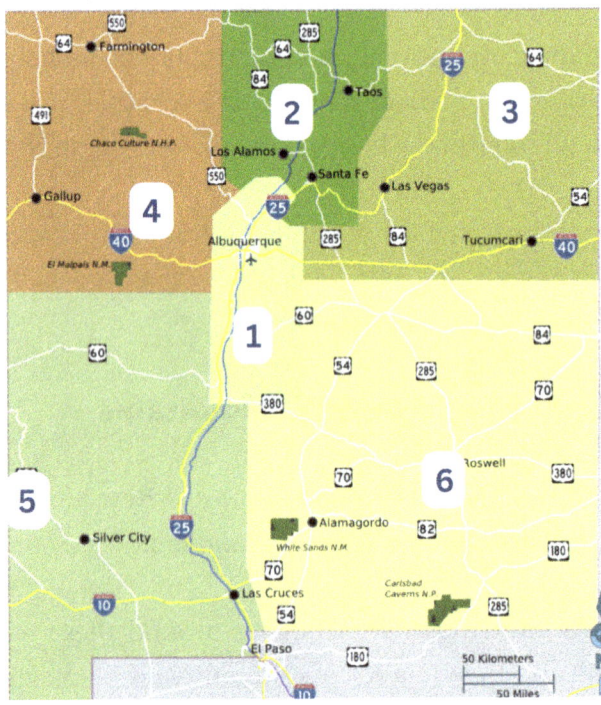

Attribution: PerryPlanet, Public domain, via Wikimedia Commons

1.	Central New Mexico	Positioned along the Center of Rio Grande Valley and home to Albuquerque. This region contains the majority of the state's population
2.	North Central New Mexico	This picturesque hilly region has many of the better-known traveler destinations of New Mexico, such as Santa Fe as well as Taos.
3.	North East New Mexico	Below, the Rocky Mountains fulfill the Great Plains. The Santa Fe Trail, and railroads, all passed through here.
4.	North West New Mexico	This area is residence to numerous unusual geological formations, red rocks, and part of the Navajo Nation.
5.	South West New Mexico	Home to picturesque low-lying hills and much of the agricultural manufacturing in the state along the Rio Grande.
6.	South East New Mexico	Elevation-wise, this is the most affordable region of the state, mostly desert yet with some unusual geologic phenomena.

Similarly, there are other raw, healthy greens you can find here. Mushrooms are another excellent wild food to look for at these higher elevations. After it rains, mushrooms sprout in many areas like the Taos Ski Valley.

Look for them around woody undergrowth, damp spots, and near streams. Mushrooms like the porcini or Boletus edulis can be seen peeking out from the ground in forests.

Porcini or Boletus edulis

(2) Chihuahuan Desert

The Chihuahuan desert gets a lot of rainfall, and the winter temperatures are cool.

Therefore, the dominant vegetation includes frost-tolerant yuccas, agaves, and grasses.

Some native plants you will find in this area are Pinon, Yucca, Agave, Globe Mallow, Desert Willow, Prickly Pear, and Mesquite.

You can also find non-native wild plants like Black Walnut, Horehound, Common Mallow, and Cattail.

Soaptree yucca (yucca elata), New Mexico

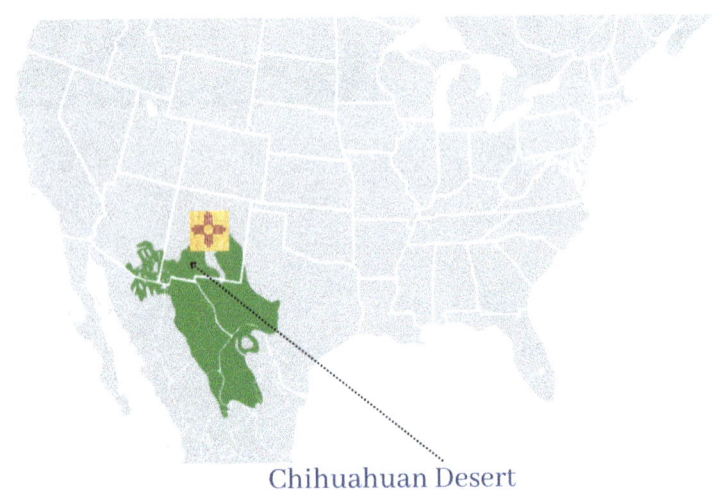

Chihuahuan Desert

Cephas, CC BY-SA 3.0 <https://creativecommons.org/licenses/by-sa/3.0>, via Wikimedia Commons

(3) Riparian Habitats

Riparian habitats are a great place to forage for wild foods like stinging nettles. This plant grows abundantly near juniper or oak trees a little further away from the river. Stinging nettle can be found between March and June in rich mountain soils of the southwest.

You should try going earlier in the morning to harvest nettles and always do this before the plant flower. One of the earliest signs of spring in these areas is the yellow-green foliage of the cottonwood trees.

Stinging Nettles   Cottonwood
Image by Eleanor Lemal from Pixabay

If you go foraging in places near the Bear Creek floodplain, it is impossible to miss these trees around that time. The inner bark of the trees can be scraped and eaten raw. The flowers, as well as the male flower catkins, are edible parts of these cottonwood trees.

Native Americans also used parts of this tree for medicinal uses like treating cuts, sprains, or insect bites

Russian olive trees are another wild plant that invades these water-loving areas around New Mexico. This thorny deciduous tree grows up to 30-40 feet and has edible berry-like olives with silver scales.

While some of the wild regions around New Mexico offer a lot of wild edibles, you can also find some within your vicinity. Wild foods grow everywhere, from your neighbor's backyard to parking lots or roadsides.

You can find wild foods anywhere if you get permission and check the legalities. Ask other local foragers where they like to go foraging and maybe accompany them on their next field trip.

Russian olive berries

5. What to Forage in New Mexico?

This chapter will help you learn how to identify some commonly found wild edible plants in New Mexico.

(1) Wild Rose

Wild Rose or the Rosa Acicularis plants belong to the Rosaceae family. These grow widely around New Mexico and are a great wild edible for foragers. You will often find these around forests with conifers, willows, or cottonwood trees.

The rose hips can be found around when summer ends, and fall starts. The best time to forage for wild rose hips is after the first frost. The natural sugars in them become sweeter in the cold. However, you can also harvest them earlier if you want. The flowers are emollient, while the leaves have astringent properties.

Rosa Acicularis

The rose hips are very high in vitamin C and flavonoids. Half an ounce of rose hips is enough for your daily-recommended vitamin C intake.

The rose hips can be plucked and dried for longer storage. However, this makes them lose a lot of the natural vitamin C. While harvesting rose petals, always leave at least one petal on the flower to allow pollination.

The plants like to grow in open areas and coastal or sandy locations. You can find them along the outsides of forests or in the mountains. Wear thick gloves to avoid being pricked by the thorns on the bushes. The fruit can easily be picked off the branches. They are great for making tea, and the citrusy flavor can be balanced with a little honey. The leaves, rose hips, and flowers are all edible. The leaves should be harvested early in spring, while the flowers should be picked in summer. This plant can also make honey, syrups, and vinegar.

Rose Hips

Rose Hip Tea

(2) Mexican Pinon

Mexican Pinon, or the Pinus Cembroides tree, is a medium-sized evergreen tree. Pinon trees grow all along the highlands of New Mexico and have edible nuts that have been sourced as food by indigenous people for a long time. The tree is the official state tree there. They grow anywhere between 15-30 feet tall and grow slowly.

The leaves or needles are long and around 1-2 inches in length. They are thick but pointed at the tips. The trees have multiple branches and thick trunks.

The nuts are usually oval and 1-3 inches long. Pinon needles are blue or blue-green and quite fragrant. The female and male flowers grow on the same plant and are pollinated by wind or insects.

The yellow flowers bloom between April and May. These trees like growing in sunny, dry areas. They like rocky or gravelly soil as well. While pinon trees can adapt to many kinds of soil, they don't favor poorly drained soil.

Pinon nuts are very rich in protein and healthy fats. The dark brown nuts are small and usually fall from the trees around summer or autumn. Once you collect the nuts, you must crack the shell and peel it open. The pale meat within this is edible. While the regular pine nuts are bland and big, these wild pinon nuts are sweet and small.

The nuts can also be ground and prepared into powder used for baking. These nuts can also be roasted before consumption and are nutritious.

Pinus Cembroides
Image by Jasminka Kovačević from Pixabay

(3) Marshmallow

Common marshmallows or the Althea Officinalis plant is a wild edible native to Europe but also found in New Mexico. This plant has been used for its medicinal properties and food for thousands of years. This perennial plant typically grows up to 100 cm but may also grow to 2 meters in the right conditions.

This plant has red or pinkish flowers with five sepals and petals. The petals and sepals are not fused. There are more than ten stamens in each flower. Marshmallow plants usually bloom between August and September. After their blooming season, round fruits appear.

The plant's roots are thick and long and taper at the ends. While the roots are yellowish-white on the outside, the inside is a fibrous white.

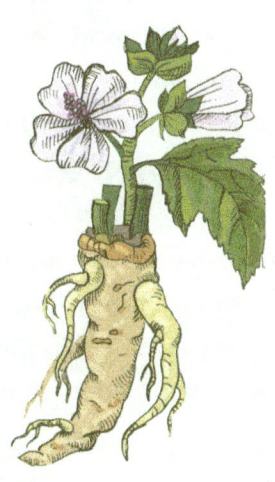

Althea Officinalis

The roots can be used for making syrup to treat respiratory issues. The roots can also be cooked like a vegetable. The leaves are edible when young and should be cooked before consumption. You can harvest the flower buds before they bloom and use them to make pickles.

(4) Sweet Clover

Sweet white clover or the Melilotus Albus grows in areas with full sun but can also tolerate partial shade. This wild plant is usually considered invasive but is great for edible foraging. Sweet clover grows in alkaline, calcium-rich, or sandy soils.

You can find it along roadsides, meadows, open fields, and mixed wood plains. This gangly plant is easy to spot and has a distinct aroma that makes it easy to identify. Sweet clover is generally biennial but may also be an annual. It belongs to the Fabaceae family, and a single plant can produce anywhere between 13,000 to 300,000 seeds.

These seeds can stay viable in the soil for decades together. The racemes of flowers and three leaflets make it easy to identify. Sweet clover flowers attract all kinds of insects, like bees, wasps, butterflies, and beetles. Beekeepers like growing this since it is a good nectar plant.

The white flowers bloom between June and October when the plant is in its second year. These small flowers are rarely larger than 5mm, and 20-50 flowers can grow on the same stalk. The tubular sweet clover flowers have petals with broader outer edges.

Three leaflets grow alternately on the stem of the plant. The fully-toothed leaflets are usually smooth but may have hairs on the surface. A distinct stalk is present on the middle leaflet. The plant can grow as tall as 3 meters.

The erect stem is smooth and may be branched or grooved. The root may produce multiple stems.

If you come across sweet clover plants, you can harvest the whole plant if you want. The leaves can be eaten raw when they are young. They have a bitter flavor and are often used in salads. You should harvest these leaves before they bloom and may even choose to cook them.

The young shoots can be cooked before consumption. The flowers are edible as well and may be cooked or consumed raw. Some people like to dry all parts of sweet clover plants and use them for making tea. The seeds are used as a spice as well. It is best to avoid consuming sweet clover too often since it can have a negative effect on liver health.

Melilotus Albus

(5) Greasewood

Greasewood, or the Sarcobatus Vermiculatus, is an edible invasive weed. This drought-tolerant plant can be found growing all around New Mexico. It grows to a height of 1-2 meters and has a long taproot.

The plant is usually identified by its small green fruits and fleshy linear leaves. The bark of the younger plants will be a whitish color that becomes gray with maturity.

The leaves are succulent and linear. They grow to around 1-4 cm and are a pale green. These leaves may grow opposite or alternately. Greasewood is a perennial native shrub that has rigid, spreading branches.

The male flowers usually grow on the same plant as the female flowers but may also grow separately. Greasewood seeds are tan or green in color and have a membranous wing. Winds usually disperse the seeds. Greasewood is unlikely to be affected by fires and still grows again due to the wind-dispersed seeds.

While many animals like prairie dogs and jackrabbits forage for this plant, it is also human food.

Native Americans have eaten the leaves and seeds of greasewood shrubs for a long time. However, the plant is poisonous to animals if they consume it in large amounts.

This is because of the presence of oxalates. It is safe for consumption in controlled amounts. You can safely cook and eat the leaves like a vegetable or add them to other dishes.

Greasewood/Sarcobatus Vermiculatus

By Cory Maylett - Personal photo, CC BY-SA 4.0, https://commons.wikimedia.org/w/index.php?curid=4973987

(6) Dandelion

Dandelion is also called lion's tooth and is a very common weed. This broadleaf plant can be found growing in many lawns around you. Dandelions adapt to most types of environments and can be found from fields to rocky hillsides.

Many people find it pesky since it tends to grow and spread fast in gardens and lawns. This plant is readily identifiable and very nutritious.

It has minerals, vitamins, and antioxidants that benefit the body. This is why you should harvest some dandelions the next time you go foraging.

The hardy perennial has a rosette base and multiple flowering stems. The plant is nutritious and has healing properties as well. This weed is good for gardens since it provides nitrogen and minerals to the soil. Dandelions also attract pollinators to your garden and help quickly ripen fruits.

The environment the plant grows in will determine how big it grows. The plants are usually around 20-30 cm tall. Around 100-200 florets can grow on a flowerhead, with no disk florets. The yellow ray florets spread as they go outwards. The bracts at the base of the flowerhead are green. The inner ones are linear and tend to form a tube around the ovaries. The outer bracts curve downward and are linear-lanceolate.

Dandelion Flower

Dandelion Honey Syrup

The roots, flowers, and leaves are all edible. The flowers can be cooked or added to various recipes. The leaves can be eaten raw or cooked. You can also dry the leaves and store them for the winter. Some people use dandelion root as a substitute for coffee. These parts can be dried and used for making dandelion tea to reap the plant's health benefits.

(7) Juniper

The one-seed juniper or Juniperus Monosperma tree flourished in the dry environment of New Mexico. The plant tends to grow quicker when there is more moisture in the air, halting its growth during drier periods.

The plants can be anywhere between 5-30 feet tall. The taproot often grows 20-30 feet long in the younger plants, while the older plants can have almost 150-200 ft long roots.

This evergreen shrub is easy to identify. It has a round, dense crown and multiple stems. The bark exfoliates in long strips and is a grayish-brown color. The coniferous plant is also multi-stemmed. The males and females grow separately. The male junipers are more yellow-brown and have tiny cones. The female juniper has berry-like seed cones. These berries only have one seed each and hence the name. They turn a bluish-purple color as they ripen. The foliage is needle-like on the younger plants but scalier on, the older junipers.

The berries are the edible part of these plants. However, it is important to harvest only a few things since they are also a food source for other animals like coyotes.

In addition, these berries have diuretic and disinfectant properties. In the past, the bark was dried and used for making tea to reduce gastrointestinal inflammation or ease childbirth.

The berries are soft and juicy with thin outer flesh. You can consume them raw or dried and ground. The powder can be used as a seasoning or for baking. Only the berries of the Juniperus Oxycedrus and Juniperus Sabina are poisonous.

Juniper or Juniperus Monosperma
By Dave Powell, USDA Forest Service, Bugwood.org - This image is Image Number 1214093 at Forestry Images, a source for forest health, natural resources and silviculture images operated by The Bugwood Network at the University of Georgia and the USDA Forest Service., CC BY-SA 3.0 us, https://commons.wikimedia.org/w/index.php?curid=3259803

(8) Trecul Yucca

Yucca Treculeana is an edible perennial shrub belonging to the Agavaceae family. It is native to New Mexico and is a popular variety of yucca. Almost all yucca plants are edible, but the thick-leaved plants are usually harvested for the fruit.

The plants can grow beyond 10 feet tall in the right conditions. The stem usually branches, and the lower part of the trunk usually has a mat of dead leaves. The upper leaves tend to grow in random directions. The leaves are dagger-shaped and top the short limbs growing from the trunk. Yucca leaves can grow 15-50 inches long and are usually 1-7 cm wide. These u-shaped leaves have a thorn at the end, and the edges are lined with coarse threads.

Trecul Yucca

The flowers bloom between April and May. The creamy-white flowers are egg-shaped and usually enclosed within thick leaves. Yucca flowers also tend to have a little red tint that makes them easy to identify. A dense spray of flowers grows on the branches of the flower stalk. The fruits mature and become seed capsules.

Please be sure to look for the plants around desert grasslands or scrubs. They adapt well to fry, sandy or rocky soils. The fruit from the thick-leaved yucca plants is the most desired edible part.

They are usually 10 cm long and can be baked or roasted before consumption. These fruits tend to taste like figs or sweet molasses. The fruit can be dried and ground to use as flour.

Yucca ground meal can last months after drying. You can also pluck the fruits before they have ripened and let them sit till they become ripe. The flower stalks should be harvested before they bloom or are tasteless. The stalks can be eaten raw when they are still tender or cooked. The flowers are also edible but only have a good flavor when picked at the right time. The stems contain toxic saponins and can thus be consumed only after cooking to remove the toxins.

(9) Banana Yucca

Banana yucca, or the Yucca baccata, has been a food source for Native Americans for centuries. It belongs to the Agavaceae family and is a popular landscape variety.

This is one of the easiest yucca plants to identify and is a perennial shrub that grows in grasslands, desert hills, and juniper woodlands. It adapts well to rocky or sandy soil types.

The basal leaves are sword-like and can grow to 10-40 inches. They grow in a dense rosette, and curling threads are on the margins. The tips of the leaves have a sharp needle that may be an inch long. This is why it is essential to handle them carefully to avoid injury.

The flowers bloom between April and July and are banana-shaped. The creamy white flowers are fleshy and egg-shaped. The fruits mature into a succulent pod that is edible.

Banana Yucca

The flower petals of the banana yucca contain a high amount of Vitamin C. The fruits can be harvested and cooked. Remove the seeds first, then bake, dry, roast, or boil the fruit. The roots are rich in saponins and can be used for preparing soap.

(10) Indian Ricegrass

Indian Ricegrass belongs to the Poaceae family and is a native bunchgrass. The plant is also called Indian millet, sand grass, or wye and is a wild edible. It is a valuable forage for cattle, but the seeds are also edible for humans.

This plant grows up to 50 cm tall and has an open sheath. The leaves are 15-30 cm long and 1-3 mm wide. The tightly rolled leaves make the plant look quite wiry. A single flower grows at the end of each thin branch. The densely Pilose lemmas are around 3 mm in length.

This plant grows well in well-drained soil and can tolerate sodic or saline soil. Indian Ricegrass can grow in desert shrubs, mixed grass prairies, and ponderosa pine forests. It is drought-tolerant as well.

Native Americans have used Indian Ricegrass as a food source for a long time. The major use was to grind the seeds and use them as flour. Foragers still collect the seeds and consume them raw or cook them like oatmeal. The ground seeds are used for baking bread or thickening soups.

Eriocoma hymenoides (Indian ricegrass /sand rice grass)
By NRCS - http://www.mt.nrcs.usda.gov/technical/ecs/plants/heritage/ricegrass.html. Public Domain, https://commons.wikimedia.org/w/index.php?curid=4265245

(11) Bee Balm

Bee balm, wild bergamot, or the Monarda fistulosa, is an edible aromatic plant that grows from creeping rhizomes. Indigenous tribes like the Ojibwa and Menominee have used this plant for a long time. It is considered especially beneficial for treating the common cold. The plant can be identified by its fuzzy flowers, which are a pink-purple color.

The round flowers are very aromatic and grow in flowerhead during mid-summer. The flowers at the center bloom before the flowers at the periphery. The corolla has an upper lip and three lower lips. Insects tend to land on the slender lower lips.

This plant is drought-resistant and tends to thrive in sunny, dry areas. Bee balm plants in moist conditions will develop mildew quite quickly. The leaves of the plant are ovate or lanceolate. They are usually light green but May also be a darker green with yellow or red tints. The margins are serrated and hairless. The leaves smell like oregano and are maybe 10 cm long. Bee balm plants can grow between 30-60 cm tall.

You will find this plant in dry or slightly moist soils with many suns. It thrives along the edges of fields, limestone glades, or thickets. They may also grow in woodlands but in limited quantities. The leaves, as well as the flowers, are edible. They can be eaten raw or cooked. The flowers can be dried and used for making tea.

Bee balm

(12) Golden Currant

Golden currant is native to New Mexico, especially in the greater Albuquerque area. When you go foraging at the beginning of spring, look for this shrub with fragrant yellow flowers. The plant is usually found in places with an elevation range between 3000-8000 feet. Golden currant plants favor full sun but can tolerate partial shade as well.

The small yellow flowers have five petals and a vanilla or clover-like aroma. The trumpet-shaped flowers tend to bloom before most other plants in spring. These flowers attract butterflies and hummingbirds. The flowers later grow into edible currants that you can harvest. The currants are initially a red color but mature into a deep blue.

The leaves are small and green in the spring. This foliage turns a bright red color by fall and then sheds. The three-lobed leaves will stay a vibrant apple-green color for longer if they get enough water.

Since golden currant is tolerant to many kinds of soil, you may find it around various areas. However, it is partial to well-drained soil. The plant grows more commonly around the margins of streams or on damp slopes.

However, this plant will not grow in soil with high salt content. When you spot the shrub, harvest the ripe berries and use them for making juices or jams if you don't want to consume them raw.

Ribes Aureum/ Golden currant
Photo by David Thielen on Unsplash

(13) Amaranth

Amaranthus Palmeri is native to New Mexico and is considered a superweed. The plant is invasive when it grows in disturbed areas but not in its natural habitat.

This nutritious plant was a popular natural food source for the Native Americans. This plant can be found in dry as well as moist soil. Look for it around desert grasslands, floodplains, roadsides, pastures, and farmland. Since the plant is adapted to desert conditions, it has a very quick lifecycle. Each plant produces thousands of seeds after it germinates. This annual plant has multiple branches growing laterally and will usually be a meter tall. The leaves, as well as the stem, have a smooth surface. The petioles on the leaves are long. The plant looks like a poinsettia because of the symmetrical arrangement of the leaves. The female and male plants are separate.

The whitish-green flowers are around 2-3 mm in size and grow in cylindrical clusters. The fruits have one seed each, and these are exposed at maturity. The leaves grow alternately and have no hairs. The young plants have lanceolate leaves, while the mature plants have ovate leaves.

Amaranth plants with red stems are usually around 1-2 meters tall. You can harvest the leaves and consume them raw or cooked. They can also be dried and stored. The dried leaves are often used for making stews or soups. The seeds are nutritious as well and can be ground into a powder. This powder can be used for baking. The gelatinous seeds cannot be crushed in your mouth directly.

Amaranthus Palmeri

(14) Echinacea

Echinacea, or the Echinacea purpurea, is an indigenous perennial plant that you can find while foraging. This plant has four different varieties and has been used for medicinal purposes by Native Americans for centuries. It is also a wild edible that can be safely consumed and is quite nutritious. The plant grows in prairies, barrens, and open woods.

One of the distinguishing features of echinacea is the daisy-like flower with a prickly seed cone. The flowers may be pink or purple. The high seed cones have sharp spines, and the florets grow around this cone. The plant is usually in bloom for a month after summer's first couple of weeks. However, some echinacea plants may lie dormant after this initial blooming period and then bloom again at the beginning of fall.

The leaves are toothed and white hairs may be on the upper surface. This is why the leaves are rough to touch. They may be ovate or lance-shaped and are usually narrow. The upper surface of the leaves will be a darker green than the lower surface. The average plant will grow up to 1 meter tall.

The flower petals, as well as the leaves, can be safely consumed raw or cooked. Other parts of the plant should only be used for medicinal use. Echinacea is a popular ingredient for preparing a natural herbal tonic for improving immunity.

Echinacea/ Echinacea Purpurea

(15) Parry's Agave

Parry's Agave, or the Agave Parryi, is an edible succulent belonging to the Asparagaceae family. You will come across wide ornate varieties of this perennial plant. The plant is generally easy to spot and identify since it grows 1-2 feet tall and is twice as wide.

These plants have a dense rosette of leaves that are sword-like and thorny. The plants can keep growing for decades, and multiple offshoots are produced. These grow up to a towering stalk that blooms and dies. In the past, tribes like the Apaches roasted the stem heart and used the fibers from the leaves for cordage.

The flowers are bright yellow, while the buds will be reddish. They bloom between June and August in a cluster of tubular flowers. These plants only bloom a single time during their lifetime. These flowers have a lot of pollen and nectar, thus attracting hummingbirds and insects. Parry's agave fruit is usually oval and an inch long. The leaves may be gray or a light green color.

The rosette may contain almost a hundred overlapping leaves. These are wide in the middle and taper to a thorny tip. The leaves are lined with vicious brown spines less than an inch apart. While foraging, you will find these plants growing in desert grasslands, granite or limestone soils, and ponderosa woodlands. The stem can be cut before the plant flowers. This will allow you to gather the honey water from the heart, and it can be fermented to make pulque like the Mexicans.

The nectar from the plant is also a great natural substitute for sugar. All the parts of Parry's agave plant are edible. The leaves are generally used for making soap since they contain saponins. However, the stems can be collected and roasted. They make for a great asparagus substitute.

Parry's Agave/Agave Parryi

(16) Chokecherry

Black chokecherry, or the Prunus virginiana, is another wild plant found while foraging in New Mexico. It is a native, deciduous shrub considered a small tree. It has multiple stems and forms a thicket.

The slender stems can either branch from the base of the shrub or the main components spread upright. Chokecherry plants can vary greatly in size since they can grow anywhere between 3-20 feet tall. In areas like the Great Basin, you may come across nearly 40 feet tall chokecherry trees.

The root system is very deep, and they have a rhizome network. The roots can extend up to 6 feet vertically and 35 feet laterally. The fruits grow as drupes, and each has a single seed. The plant flowers between the end of May and the beginning of June.

They leaf out towards the end of spring and flower a couple of weeks after that. The fruits from the plant will mature towards the end of summer but spoil fast.

Black chokecherry

Mushrooms of New Mexico

Mushrooms rely on dampness. In the desert, if there's no downpour, there're no mushrooms. Yet in a great year, when the rainfalls come, and the temperatures are perfect, the loss can be an efficient mushroom season in northern New Mexico.

If you want to hunt for (and consume) wild mushrooms securely, below are some fundamental newbies' guidelines.

- Never eat a mushroom; you're not 100 percent sure. That's basic and must regulation for all wild edibles, yet the risks are incredibly high with mushrooms because some are poisonous when consumed.

- Make a spore print. Several mushrooms look similar on the outside, and a spore print will aid you in differentiating amongst types.

- Cook your mushrooms well. The cell walls of mushrooms are made of chitin, not cellulose.

- Join a regional mushroom club. You can find out about the New Mexico Mycological Society.

(1) Oyster

Oyster mushrooms are a common mushroom found in New Mexico. They obtain their name from their oyster shell-like form and can be seen growing on trees, logs, or stumps. Oyster mushrooms are edible and have a somewhat sweet preference. Therefore, they can be used in soups, stir-fries, and other meals when cooked.

While these mushrooms are generally considered safe to eat, some people might experience an allergy after eating them. Follow all safety rules and if eating for the first time, take a small amount and wait some time to check the reaction.

It is vital to ensure that oyster mushrooms are cooked well before eating them, as raw oyster mushrooms can cause stomach upset.

In general, oyster mushrooms are an addition to your diet. Nevertheless, as with all mushrooms, you must take caution and consult your doctor if you have any issues.

Oyster Mushrooms

(2) Chanterelle

The chanterelle is a typical mushroom in New Mexico. This mushroom typically grows in areas with damp dirt near streams or rivers. Chanterelles are usually found in the wild, but you can grow them in-house.

These mushrooms have a distinctive, slightly fruity odor and a golden-yellow color. Chanterelles are considered to be exquisite mushrooms, and they are often made use of in premium cuisine.

When cooked, chanterelles have a fragile taste called nutty or earthy.

Chanterelles are an excellent source of vitamins and minerals, consisting of potassium, copper, and iron. They likewise consist of numerous antioxidants that may provide wellness advantages.

Chanterelle

(3) King Bolete

The King Bolete is a common mushroom discovered in New Mexico. This mushroom is characterized by its large size and also its brownish cap. The King Bolete generally grows in areas with many trees, such as forests.

This mushroom is edible, yet it can be quite difficult to chew due to its thick flesh. Therefore, when cooking the King Bolete, it's ideal to cut it thin to ensure that it can be chewed and eaten well.

King Bolete

Image by Pexels from Pixabay

(4) Lobster Mushrooms

Lobster mushrooms are just one of the most common mushrooms in New Mexico. They are generally found expanding on trees, logs, or dead leaves. These mushrooms have a reddish-brown color and a weighty texture.

They obtain their name from their lobster-like appearance as well as their preference. Lobster mushrooms can be eaten raw or cooked. When cooking lobster mushrooms, it is best to sauté them or cook them.

How to recognize them:

- Color: orange to reddish-orange colored on the outside with white tinted flesh on the inside;
- Fragrance: a fish and shellfish fragrance; a warped cap that is occasionally split that resembles a vessel or upside-down pyramid
- Gills: no gills - blunt ridges with tiny pimples instead of gills; and grows in the fall, generally after rainfalls.

The only caveat for eating lobster mushrooms is not to collect old specimens and not to let harvested mushrooms relax long before they can spoil. Some individuals likewise appear to be sensitive.

The strategy to eat this is to take caution the first time, as everybody's body varies. Eat a little of the mushroom each time and also see just how you feel.

Lobster Mushrooms

(5) Puffball

Puffballs are common in New Mexico. These mushrooms have a round or oval form, usually white or cream-colored. They release a smoke of spores when they mature or duplicate, hence the name Puffball.

Puffballs are edible when young and still have a solid inside. However, once they create a hollow cavity at the center, they are appropriate to consume.

It is best to slice them very finely so they can cook evenly. These mushrooms can be sauteed, grilled, or roasted, making an excellent addition to any dish.

While the majority of puffballs are not poisonous, a couple of similar species can be unsafe if consumed. The false puffball looks similar to the edible selection however has a little hole at the top where the spores are released.

This mushroom is poisonous as well as ought not to be eaten. Another look-alike is the amanita mushroom, which is poisonous. If you are unsure, leave it!

Puffballs/Lycoperdon perlatum

MUSHROOM ANATOMY

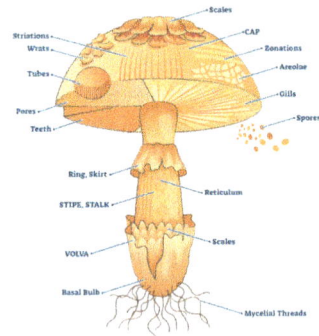

Cap

The top part of the mushroom is known as the cap or the pileus. Whenever you look at the mushroom, this is the first thing that will catch your eye. It is an umbrella or a dome-like structure that protects the spores and gills from the elements.

Gills

Mushrooms have gills that look pretty similar to those of fish. Gills refer to fine teeth-like structures that can be found right under the cap of the mushroom and house their spores.

Spores

Pores are also known as spores and are a means of propagation for mushrooms. Spores are present in the gills.

Mycelium

The roots of plants usually dig deep into the ground to find the nutrition they require. Even mushrooms have fine hair-like strands that dig into the soil to obtain the nutrients they need. These structures are known as mycelium. The function of mycelium in mushrooms is the same as roots in plants. The fine filament-like structures the mycelium is made of are known as hyphae.

Fruiting Body

The entire mushroom that grows from the mycelium is referred to as its fruiting body, and it contains the cap, gills, volva, stipe, and veil.

Stipe

This is also known as the stem of the mushrooms, and it's the vertical portion upon which the cap sits. It is also visible above the surface.

Ring

The ring is the annulus of the mushroom and is a small part of the veil left behind on its stem. As the cap matures, it breaks through the veil, and the leftover pieces in this process form a ring-like structure around the stipe.

Veil

It is an additional layer of protection that ensures the spores are safe while the mushroom is maturing.

Volva

The cap-like structure most mushrooms have close to the base is known as the volva. This is also the leftover bit of the veil that homes the spores.

Seasonal Calendar of Mushrooms in South West United States

Season	Mushroom	Other Information
Spring	Morel	Yellow and black morels are found in Texas in spring and are located in damp areas, around dying or dead sycamore, elm trees, ash trees, and shed sites under conifers. A lot more seldom, morels have been found in the autumn west of Austin, near the Pedernales River.
Summer	Chanterelles	Chanterelle has a funnel-shaped cap which the stem combines into. Chanterelles can be found in woodlands with a lot of oaks and conifers. Chanterelles are potentially one of the most abundant mushrooms in the Southern Appalachia area.
Summer	Black Trumpet	Black Trumpets are the most difficult to locate of all the mushrooms in Texas. Commonly, hunters look for this mushroom in woodlands, particularly in areas with lots of oak and beech, along hillsides where water runs or washes down the hill, and along creek edges.
Summer	Boletes	You can find many species within the Boletaceae family members. The one pictured above is the striking Shaggy Stalked Bolete. Aureoboletus Betula is edible! Make sure to get your ID abilities down for this one, as not all family members are edible.
Summer	Chicken of the Woods	Chicken of the woods or Laetiporus sulphureus is also known as the sulfur polypore. These mushrooms are an excellent replacement for chicken due to their meaty texture. You will spot them in tier-like clusters on the stumps and trunks of oak, willow, chestnut, yew, and cherry trees. They do not have a discernible stem and grow in clusters.
Autumn	Berkeley's Polypore	Not the top edible mushroom, yet still a delightful one to locate because of its size. These Berkeley's Polypores can grow to a massive dimension, like 1-1/2 ft. long. When they are young, they are also simple to cut; Berkeley's polypore can be eaten.
Autumn	Hen of the Woods	This fungus can be discovered expanding at the base of huge old trees. Thus, it is often typical in historical districts with large old oak trees. It tastes delicious, and it's not unusual to locate huge flushes of them.

Season	Mushroom	Other Information
Autumn	Oyster Mushroom	An incredibly bountiful mushroom throughout numerous parts of the Southeast, the Oyster mushroom. This gilled saprobic fungus can be found in small to huge collections breaking out of the wood of dead or dying trees.
	Lion's Mane	Lions Mane mushroom chooses dead hardwood as an all-natural environment. Oak, walnut, beech, maple, and also sycamore trees are all optimal for this fungus. Not just does this mushroom taste delicious, but it's also helpful for you. Lion's mane mushrooms include bioactive materials that benefit the body, especially the mind, heart, and also intestine.
Winter	Wood Blewit	The earliest description came from P. Bulliard in 1790 and was additionally known as Tricholoma nudum earlier. You can find them in both coniferous as well as deciduous forests. It is a relatively distinct mushroom that is also eaten, though care should be taken regarding edibility. It can be found naturally fruiting during winter months in Central Texas.
	Enoki	Enoki mushrooms (Flammulina velutipes), additionally referred to as enokitake mushrooms, are a common cold-weather mushroom that's easy to locate just about anywhere in the globe. Be aware that enoki do have dangerous hazardous look-a-likes, and also they can just be favorably related to a spore print. Be extremely cautious when collecting this mushroom in the wild!
	Winter Oyster	As the name suggests, North American winter months oyster mushrooms are located between November and March, possibly October via April in cooler years. Winter oyster mushrooms expand specifically on wood. Anything with a brown or rusty spore print. The time of year should eliminate the potentially hazardous Pholiota and Gymnopilus varieties, yet dangerous galerinas (Galerina marginata) do fruit in winter.

6. How to Store Foraged Goods

An essential skill for foragers to learn is storing wild foods. You will often find yourself carrying home a large bounty that you cannot possibly finish in a day or two. It is also important to keep some food in storage for the winter or learn to store your favorite edibles for the off-season.

This is why you must focus on cleaning and storing your foraged goods properly to make them last as long as possible. This chapter will help you learn simple ways to clean and store foraged wild edibles effectively.

Cleaning Foraged Plants

When you go foraging and identify some wild plants, pick only as much as you need. Throw away any extra parts and leave them to decompose on the ground. Dust or wipe off as much dirt as you can there as well.

This will make it easier for you to clean the rest when you go home. It will also help you check whether some parts are spoiled or damaged under the dirt so you can leave them behind in the wild instead of carrying them home. You can carry some clean paper towels or a toothbrush to help you do this. This is the first step of basic cleaning when you are foraging.

Once you take the wild plants home, clean them properly. Place them in a colander and rinse them in the sink under some running water.

cleaning your foraged plants

You can scrub off any tough dirt stuck on parts like the roots. The water will usually wash the rest off. Use cold water for this, and avoid washing them for too long. Some greens can wilt if kept wet. Other parts can be cleaned by soaking them in a water tub for 10-15 minutes. This will allow the dirt to settle at the base.

Once you wash off the dirt from your wild plants, use some clean towels and pat them dry. Unless you intend to cook them, the plant parts should be as dry as possible. This is because moisture will cause them to spoil faster and attract mold. There needs to be more than just patting the plants dry since they absorb water while washing them. Spread a few paper towels or newspapers and allow the foraged plants to dry for about 30 minutes. You can also spin them in a salad spinner a few times to dry them out as much as possible. The more effectively you remove excess water, the better the foraged food will store.

Storing Foraged Goods

After you have cleaned all the foraged plants, set aside the food you intend to consume that day or over the next couple of days, these foods can be kept on the counter or stored in containers or paper bags in the fridge till you use them.

Some fresh wild foods like burdock roots will keep well for 2-3 months without any extra steps. However, other foods like wild greens or mushrooms will spoil quickly. The rest will have to be preserved and stored for later use.

There are many ways foraged plants can be stored for long periods, and many of these methods have been carried out since ancient times but are still as effective.

One tip is to research the best storage method for the specific wild food you want to store. For example, while certain herbs are best preserved by drying, some greens are better stored by blanching and freezing. Similarly, some methods are specifically meant for a particular type of wild food.

Dehydrate

As mentioned before, removing moisture helps keep food without spoiling it for longer. This is how dehydration works, removing all the moisture from the foraged food. Dehydration can be done in a few different ways.

One simple and old way is to dry the plant parts under the sun. This is usually how herbs are dried. For example, you can tie a bunch of herbs in a bundle and hang them outside under partial shade.

Dehydrate

This will allow them to dry out soon, and the herbs can be used for months without spoilage. The other more convenient way is to get yourself a dehydrator. These appliances are inexpensive and a must in a forager's kitchen.

Plant parts can be cut and spread on a dehydrator and allowed to dry out. The settings may differ depending on your chosen appliance, but you generally have to set a temperature and time while the dehydrator does the rest. These dehydrated foods can then be stored in airtight bags or jars. Depending on the plant part, they may sometimes last months to a couple of years. Some dried plant foods are also ground into a powder for use as a spice, thickener, or flour.

Freeze

Freezing is another great way to store many wild foods. Some wild foods can be frozen directly, while others may have to be blanched before you freeze them.

Always clean the foods properly before you freeze them. You can chop up the plant parts and store them in freezer bags. You can also spread them on a baking sheet and place them in the freezer to freeze for a while before transferring them into freezer bags for storage.

Certain wild foods, such as mushrooms, must be cooked first and then frozen to keep them from spoiling. You can also grind some wild foods into a paste and pour them into ice cube trays to freeze. These cubes are a great way to add the ingredients to soups or stews later.

Freezing

Ferment

Fermentation is another great way to store foods for longer. It is the oldest way of preserving food and is still practiced worldwide. This is how delicious foods like kimchi and sauerkraut are prepared. This method allows you to preserve wild foods for longer, and these preparations are also great for your digestive system.

It usually involves the use of simple ingredients like vinegar and salt. You can look up fermentation recipes for the specific wild food you want to preserve and follow the process to ferment them successfully. These fermented foods will usually stay in the fridge for a few months.

These simple methods will help you avoid food wastage to a large extent. Always preserve the foods as soon as possible once you get them home. It is also important to clean everything properly before you store them. Another simple tip is only to harvest what you will need. Please don't pick a lot of wild food to let it go into the bin later.

Mushroom Fermentation

Storing Foraged Plants

Many foraging books are centered around mushrooms as they are often difficult to identify, find, and store, but they are chock full of nutrients. This is why they are often sold at a much steeper price than other foraged plants. Ramps and nettles are the only plants that can compare with mushrooms' rising prices.

But this does not mean that the leafy plants should be ignored. They are often a great addition to salads; some pack an explosion of taste. They can also be used as seasonings and added to stews, soups, and everything else you can imagine.

The problem with foraging wild greens is that they do not last long. It is necessary to clean, process, and store them properly so that you can enjoy them for a long time. This section of this chapter will cover important details regarding the storage of various plants.

Difference Between Wild and Store-bought Greens

While you may think that both store-bought greens and the greens that you forage yourself are the same, many differences exist between them that separate them.

Foraged greens are often healthier, safer, and cheaper as they are free. You will be surprised to know that the greens you gather in the wild often last much longer than those you buy in the store. For instance, lamb quarters can last for almost three weeks in the refrigerator. Similarly, spruce tips can last for nearly a month.

Storing Mushrooms

Canned Mushroom

Pickled Mushroom

Mushroom Powder

Amaranth, nettles, sochan, and various other greens can stay fresh and usable for almost a month. Burdock stalks can remain good for a couple of months and are still usable for up to 3-4 months. Compared to these, salad greens you buy from the store go bad in just a few days.

You are mistaken if you put the herbs in paper bags and expect them to last long in your home refrigerator. It would help if you trapped some moisture along with the plants to keep them suitable for a long. Here are some tips that can help you have fresh greens for a long time.

Tips

Always pick the greens as early as possible in the day. It is recommended to pick them up before the sun rises. Plants often have little drops of dew on them before sunrise. This added moisture can help you to carry them a long distance. You can also drink this dew, as it is safe in most places.

Once you return home, put the greens in separate breathable containers or paper bags. Do not cramp the greens, and let enough space between the stalks to ensure proper airflow.
Now refrigerate the greens immediately.

Do not store any plants without cleaning them thoroughly. If you uprooted the whole plant, you could also soak the plant with roots in cold water. This will freshen up the plant.

Storing in Plastic

You can also use plastic containers to store the greens but only in rare circumstances.

Plastic can conserve much heat, which can harm plants. Only store your greens in plastic for a short time, such as when transporting them from where you foraged them to your house.

Delicate Greens: Harvesting and Storing

Delicate greens and flowers are fragile and may break or disintegrate if mishandled.

Therefore, carrying small containers to store these when you go foraging is recommended. You can also surround them with large leaves, which will act as natural bubble wrap and create a buffer, so the flowers don't get damaged.

You can also put damp towels in the containers and use them to store delicate flowers. In this case, using plastic is fine. But always refrigerate the plants as soon as you get home, as delicate flowers wilt quickly.

As mentioned earlier, soaking is an essential step that you must perform after rinsing the plants clean. Soaking or submerging the plants in ice-cold water can remove the debris, dirt, and insects (if any) and refresh the plants. As a result, they will become perky, fresh, and crisp again- almost akin to when you picked them.

Once you have soaked the plants, you can follow the remaining steps of the cleaning process. Putting the greens directly in the refrigerator won't last long, especially if you store them in a paper bag. Thus, the first step of storing should constantly be cleaning, rinsing, washing, and soaking.

Harvesting and Storing

7. Let's Cook – Edible Wild Plant Recipes

Note: Clean the plants very well after harvesting them. Wipe them with a moist paper towel. If the soil is stuck on them, rinse it.

(1) Shrimp With Red Chile And Pinon Nuts

Serves: 3 – 4

Ingredients:

- 1 pound medium-large shrimp in the shell, peeled, deveined
- 1/3 – ½ cup medium-hot New Mexico chili powder
- 1 cup pinon nuts
- 1 ½ tablespoon heavy whipping cream
- ½ teaspoon kosher salt or to taste
- 2 cloves garlic, crushed, minced
- ¼ cup extra-virgin olive oil
- 2 tablespoons honey
- ¼ cup coarsely chopped cilantro

Directions:

- Place a heavy, dry pan over medium-high heat. Add pinon nuts and toast the nuts, constantly stirring, until slightly golden brown.

- Stir in garlic. Keep constantly stirring until dark golden brown. Make sure you do not burn the nuts and garlic. So if necessary, raise the pan about 2 inches over the flame.

- Pour oil and mix well. When the oil is slightly hot, add shrimp and mix well. Now add chili powder and stir.

- Stir in honey and heavy cream. Once the shrimp cooks, turn off the heat. Add salt and stir.

- Sprinkle cilantro on top and serve.

Shrimp With Red Chile And Pinon Nuts

(2) Black Greasewood With Tofu

Serves: 2 – 3

Ingredients:

- 1 cup black greasewood leaves + extra to finish
- 2 cups cubed tofu
- ½ teaspoon salt or to taste
- ¼ teaspoon pepper or any spice blend of your choice
- 1 teaspoon soy sauce or liquid aminos
- 1 tablespoon olive oil or more if required

Directions:

- Before you cut the tofu into cubes, press the tofu of excess moisture. For this, place tofu over layers of paper towels. Place some paper towels over the tofu. Keep something heavy over the tofu, as a cold drink can. Let the excess moisture drain for about 20 minutes.

- Pour oil into a pan and let it heat over medium heat. When the oil is hot, add tofu to the pan. Mix well into the oil. Add more oil if required. Let it cook for a couple of minutes.

- Scatter black greasewood leaves and cook until the tofu is brown and crisp. Stir every 2 – 3 minutes. The leaves may crisp up in the process of cooking.

- Add salt, pepper, and soy sauce and mix well. Add some more greasewood leaves and mix well. Turn off the heat and serve.

Black Greasewood With Tofu

(3) Prickly Pear And Lime Sorbet

Serves: 3 – 4

Ingredients:

- ¾ pound ripe prickly pears halved lengthwise
- ½ tablespoon fresh lime juice
- ½ tablespoon mezcal (optional)
- 1/3 cup amber agave nectar
- 1 tablespoon grated lime zest

Directions:

- Use a spoon, scoop the flesh from the prickly pear halves, and put them into a blender.

- Blend until very smooth.

- Place a fine wire mesh strainer over a bowl and pour the blended mixture into the strainer. Discard the seeds.

- Pour the blended fruit into a bowl. Stir in lime juice, agave, mescal, and lime zest.

- Keep the bowl covered in the refrigerator for 4 to 5 hours or until very chilled.

- Churn the sorbet in an ice cream maker following the manufacturer's instructions.

- Once the sorbet is ready, transfer it into a freezer-safe container and freeze until use.

- If you do not have an ice cream maker, after step 5, pour the mixture into a freezer-safe container and freeze for 2 hours. Stir well and place it back in the freezer.

- Repeat this process of freezing and stirring hourly until the sorbet is set.

Prickly Pear And Lime Sorbet

(4) Stinging Nettle Stew

Serves:: 8 – 9

Ingredients:

- 10 chicken drumsticks and thighs
- 5 – 6 cups water or as required
- 2 large onions, diced
- 2 cups New Mexico salsa
- 4 – 5 tablespoons olive oil
- 7 – 8 cloves roasted garlic or to taste
- 1/3 cup finely grated fresh ginger
- 12 – 16 cups stinging nettles, rinsed, drained, chopped
- 1 teaspoon salt or more to taste
- 1 teaspoon pepper or more to taste
- 18 – 20 shiitake mushrooms, discard stems

To serve: Optional
- New Mexico goat cheese
- Basil pesto
- Sour dough bread

Directions:

- Place a soup pot over medium heat. Add half the oil. When the oil is hot, add chicken and cook until brown.

- Stir in the mushrooms. Pour enough water to cover the chicken and mushrooms. When the mixture starts boiling, turn the heat to low heat and cook for about 2 hours.

- As the water in the pot reduces, add more. Turn off the heat.

- Could you remove the chicken and mushrooms from the pot, and do not discard the broth?

- Cut the mushrooms into slices. Remove the bones from the chicken.

- Add chicken and mushrooms back into the pot.

- Place a pan over medium heat. Add remaining oil. Add onions and ginger when the oil is hot and cook until onions are light brown. Transfer the onion mixture to the soup pot. Place the soup pot over medium heat.

- Add salsa, stinging nettles (ensure you wear gloves while picking and cleaning them. This is important.), salt, garlic, and pepper.

- Mix well. Cook on low for about 20 minutes, stirring occasionally.

- Serve in bowls with suggested serving options.

Stinging Nettle Stew

(5) Dandelion Greens Salad

Makes:: 2 – 3

Ingredients:

- 2 cups fresh dandelion greens
- ½ tablespoon salt
- 1 scallion or wild onion, chopped
- 1 blood orange, peeled, separated into segments, and chopped
- Water as required
- ¼ cup chopped walnuts

For the dressing:

- 1 tablespoon blood orange juice
- 1/8 teaspoon salt
- ¼ cup extra-virgin olive oil
- 1 tablespoon orange juice
- 1/8 teaspoon freshly cracked pepper or to taste

Directions:

- Blend the dressing ingredients in a blender until well combined. Pour into a bowl. Cover and set aside for a while for the flavors to meld.

- Toast the walnuts in an oven or a dry pan on your stove. Let the walnuts cool completely.

- Add salt to a pot of cold water and add dandelion greens to it. Let the greens soak for about 5 minutes. Drain well.

- Rinse the greens well in cold water. Drain well. Pat them with paper towels to remove any extra moisture.

- Put the dandelion greens into a bowl. Add walnuts, scallions, and oranges and toss well.

- Pour dressing 5 minutes before serving and toss well. Let the salad rest for 5 minutes.

Dandelion Greens Salad

(6) Rose Hip Tea

(This tea is rich in vitamin C and helps overcome flu and cold. It is also beneficial for kidney problems, obesity, relief from back pain, leg pain, etc.)

Serves: 1-2

Ingredients:

- 2 cups water
- 1 tablespoon sugar or to taste
- 2 tablespoons dried rose hips

Directions:

- Boil water in a saucepan. Stir in rose hips and turn down the heat to medium-low heat. Cover the saucepan.

- Cook for about 7 – 8 minutes. Stir occasionally.

- Stir in sugar and once the sugar dissolves, turn off the heat. Cover the saucepan and let it steep for 5 minutes.

- Strain the tea into a cup and serve.

- This can be had hot, warm, or at room temperature.

Rose Hip Tea

(7) Honey Mesquite Jelly

Makes: 1 jar

Ingredients:

- 4 cups broken mesquite bean pods
- 1/8 cup lemon juice
- ½ box (from a 1.75 ounces box) of pectin
- 3 cups water
- 2 ¼ cups granulated sugar
- 1/8 teaspoon butter

- Place the canning jar, lid, and ring in the dishwasher and run the hot water cycle. You can also sterilize it in a pot of boiling water for 5 minutes. Put them on a kitchen towel.

- Add water and mesquite pods into a pot and place the pot over high heat. Let it boil rapidly for 5 minutes. Turn off the burner. Keep the pot covered with a lid and let it infuse for an hour.

- Place a strainer over a bowl and pour the mixture into the strainer. Discard the pods. The infused water should be around 1 ½ cups.

- Pour the infused water into the pot. Stir in pectin. Place the pot over medium heat.

- When it starts boiling, stir in the sugar and lemon juice. Let it boil quickly.

- After boiling rapidly for a minute, turn off the heat. Transfer the mixture to the jar. Make sure to leave a headspace of ¼ inch.

- Clean the rim of the jar with paper towels. Put the ring and lid and fasten until the finger is tight and not too tight. If you do not want to use the jelly immediately, you need not process the jars in a canner. Refrigerate the jelly.

- Label the jar with the name and date. Store in a cool and dry place. It can last for 2 years.

- Once you open the jar, keep it in the refrigerator. It can last for 3 months. You can also freeze an opened jar for up to 6 months.

Mesquite Bean Pods

Image by Michael from Pixabay

Mesquite Jelly

Photo by Yulia Khlebnikova on Unsplash

(8) Chokecherry Barbecue Sauce

Serves: 1 – 2 jars

Ingredients:

- 1 ¾ pound chokecherries
- ½ teaspoon black mustard seed
- 1 whole clove
- ¼ cup raw sugar or honey
- ½ teaspoon red wine vinegar
- ½ tablespoon blackstrap molasses
- 6 tablespoons water
- 12 – 14 black peppercorns
- ½ small onion, minced
- 1/8 teaspoon fish sauce
- ¼ teaspoon salt

Directions:

- Mix water and chokecherries in a heavy pot and place it over medium-low heat.

- Let it cook until the berries are ruptured. Turn off the heat.

- Place a fine wire mesh strainer over a bowl. Pour the berries into the strainer and strain the berries into the bowl. About one ¼ cup of strained berries should be there.

- Pour the strained berries into a small heavy pan and place the pan over medium-low heat.

- Crush the whole spices (clove, peppercorns, and mustard) lightly and put them in a spice bag. Tie the bag and drop it into the pan. Mix well.

- Add sugar, vinegar, molasses, fish sauce, and salt, and mix well.

- Turn down the heat to low heat and let it cook for about 30 to 40 minutes or until thickened, as per your preference. Remember, the sauce will thicken further on cooling.

- Discard the spice bag. Blend the sauce with an immersion blender if desired. This is optional.

- Pour into a jar. Let it cool completely. Label the jar with the name and date and place it in the refrigerator. It can last for about two weeks. You can also can the jar if you want to keep it longer. The canning process is given in the recipe - Honey Mesquite Jelly.

Chokecherry Barbecue Sauce

(9) Yellow Sweet Clover Lemonade

Serves: 7 - 8

Ingredients:

- 2 handfuls of sweet yellow clover flowers
- 8 cups water
- 6 tablespoons sugar or to taste

Directions:

- Pour water into a pitcher. Stir in the sugar. Once the sugar dissolves completely, add sweet clover flowers.

- Give it a good stir. Cover and chill for 8 – 10 hours.

- Strain and serve.

Yellow Sweet Clover Lemonade

(10) Herbal Cough Syrup

Serves: 1 – 2 bottles

Ingredients:

- 1/8 cup grindelia
- 1/8 cup elecampane root
- 1/8 cup wild cherry bark
- 1/8 Echinacea root
- ½ teaspoon licorice root
- ¼ cup marshmallow root
- 1 tablespoon minced fresh thyme
- 1 sprig of fresh rosemary
- ¼ cup mullein leaves
- 1 cup honey
- 2 cups cold water
- ½ cup brandy or vodka or any cane alcohol (optional)
- 1 teaspoon grated orange zest

Directions:

- Add water, wild cherry bark, orange peel, grindelia, elecampane, Echinacea, and licorice roots into a pot and stir.

- Boil the mixture on a high flame.

- Turn down the heat to let it cook for about 20 – 25 minutes.

- Turn off the heat. Stir in marshmallow root and mullein leaves. Let the mixture rest for an hour.

- Place cheesecloth over a bowl and strain the mixture into the bowl. Discard the solids.

- When the mixture is lukewarm, stir in the honey and brandy.

- Pour into sterilized bottles. Label the bottles with name, date, and dosage. You can have 1 tablespoon of syrup twice a day. Keep the bottles in the refrigerator.

Herbal Cough Syrup

8. Conclusion

Thank you for buying this book. I hope you found it informative and valuable.

You can begin your foraging adventure in New Mexico and find a lot of safe, edible wild food.

Now that you know where and what to look for, you will find it a rewarding experience. Use the information given here to help you find the common wild plants growing all around New Mexico.

Practice ethical foraging and consistently identify the plants accurately before consuming them. Many lookalike plants are toxic and can cause adverse reactions or even be fatal.

You can harvest delicious wild edibles if you practice foraging carefully. Engage with other foragers or communities around you to get started. You will soon be an expert forager yourself!

Thank you, and good luck, forager!

Appendix - 1- Keep in Mind while Foraging

- Never consume any wild plant or fungi you can not determine are 100% sure. It also suggested cross-verifying with an expert if similar poisonous plants/fungi exist.

- Always remember that consuming the incorrect plant can cause health problems or, in unusual scenarios, even death.

- For example, Half of all red berries are toxic!

- Make sure to use foraged foods in small quantities in case of an upset stomach.

- See to it that the location you are foraging is safe. Know ecological threats in your foraging area, such as Wildlife, e.g., snakes, etc., chemical dangers from old oil areas, roadways, lead paint around old structures, and swamps.

- Do not destroy plants or over forage (pick only what you need). Plants are food for wild animals and have various other environmental objectives.

- Gather information and familiarize yourself with the area you are going to forage.

- Bring field guides together with you for those areas.

Appendix - 2- Foraging tour & classes in New Mexico

(1) Ellen Zachos (The Backyard Forager)- Santa Fe Area

- Edible plant walks and private wild foods & cooking classes.
- Website: backyardforager.com

(2) Albuquerque Herbalism-Albuquerque

- Classes in bioregional herbalism and medicinal plants.
- Website: https://albuquerqueherbalism.com

(3) Dryland Wilds - Vallecitos

- workshops on sustainable wildcrafting, desert perfume making, handcrafting botanical soaps, and more.
- Website: https://www.drylandwilds.com

(4) New Mexico Mycological Society -Placitas

- Know about wild mushrooms and fungi located in Placitas, New Mexico.
- Website: https://nmms.wildapricot.org

(5) Return to Nature

- You can join classes and workshops and educate people about wild plants and mushroom foraging, herbalism, survival skills, and theories about nature.
- Website: http://returntonature.us

Appendix - 3- Edible Mushrooms

EDIBLE MUSHROOMS SET

| CEP | CHAMPIGNONS | AGARIC | OYSTER | SUILLUS |

| CORAL MILKY CAR | PORCINI | RUSSULA | LACTARIUS | ASPEN |

| CAESAR'S | MOREL | SAFFRON | SHIITAKE | CHANTERELLE |

| BLACK TRUFFLE | ENOKI | INDIGO LACTARIUS | LION'S MANE MUSHROOM | PUFFBALL |

Appendix - 4 - Spore Print

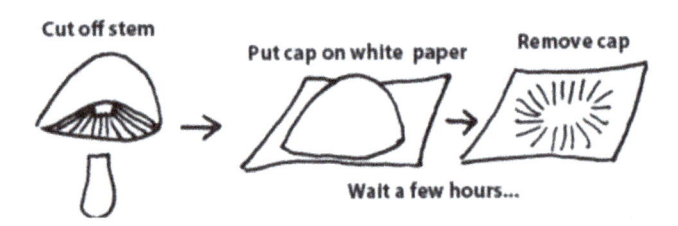

Cut off stem → Put cap on white paper → Remove cap

Wait a few hours...

The Mushroom

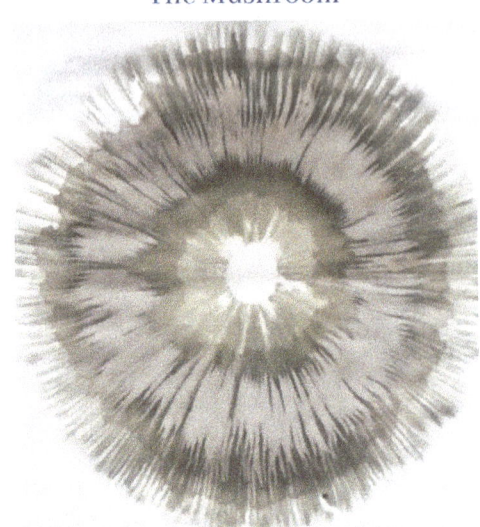

Spore Print

88

Appendix - 5- Mushroom Identification Logbook

General Details

Date/Day _____

Weather ☐ ☐ ☐

Location/GPS _____

Temprature _____

By/Person _____

Growth Medium & Surrounding

Forest Type: ☐ Coniferous ☐ Tropical ☐ Deciduous ☐ Others

Remarks _____

Growth Medium: ☐ Soil ☐ Grass ☐ Dead Wood ☐ Tree ☐ Leaf ☐ Rocky Surface ☐ Mushroom ☐ Other

Remarks _____

Soil Type: ☐ Clay ☐ Sandy ☐ Loam ☐ Others

Additional Information

Species/Type _____   Color _____

Specimen _____   Length _____

Cap Shape and Characterstics

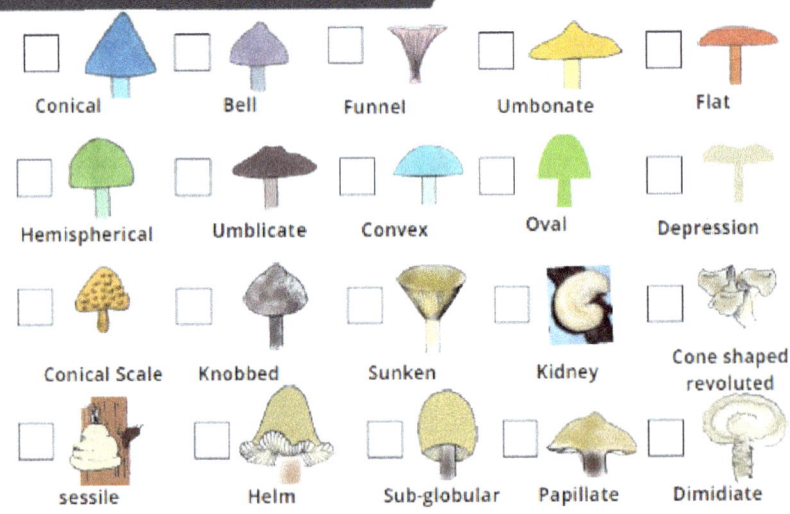

- ☐ Conical
- ☐ Bell
- ☐ Funnel
- ☐ Umbonate
- ☐ Flat
- ☐ Hemispherical
- ☐ Umblicate
- ☐ Convex
- ☐ Oval
- ☐ Depression
- ☐ Conical Scale
- ☐ Knobbed
- ☐ Sunken
- ☐ Kidney
- ☐ Cone shaped revoluted
- ☐ sessile
- ☐ Helm
- ☐ Sub-globular
- ☐ Papillate
- ☐ Dimidiate

Additional Cap Information

Cap Diagram

Other details

Cap color ....

Cap shape ....

Cap texture ....

Cap diameter ....

Cap length ....

Hymenium ....

Cap surface

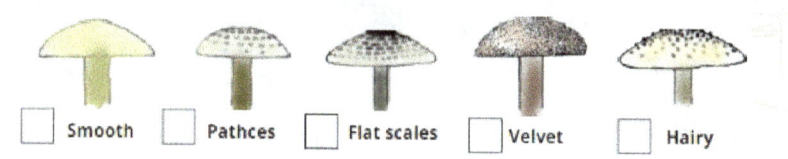

- [ ] Smooth
- [ ] Pathces
- [ ] Flat scales
- [ ] Velvet
- [ ] Hairy

Gills

- [ ] False Gills
- [ ] Teeth
- [ ] Pores
- [ ] Gills

- [ ] Close
- [ ] Spaced
- [ ] Intermediate
- [ ] Anastomosing

Additional Notes

Gill attachment to the stalk

Example of free gill attachment

☐ **Free** (Not attached)

☐ **Adnexed** (Narrowly attached)

☐ **Sinuate** (Notched before slightly running down)

☐ **Subdecurrent** (Gills running slightly down the stem)

☐ **Emarginate** Notched before attachment

☐ **Adnate** Widely attached

☐ **Decurrent** (Running down)

☐ **Seceding** (Gills attached but breaking away)

Sketch

Additional Notes

Stem Shape

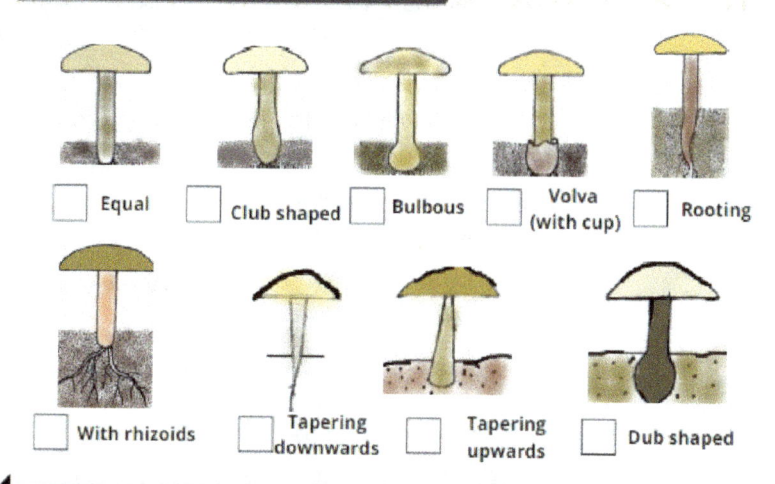

- [ ] Equal
- [ ] Club shaped
- [ ] Bulbous
- [ ] Volva (with cup)
- [ ] Rooting
- [ ] With rhizoids
- [ ] Tapering downwards
- [ ] Tapering upwards
- [ ] Dub shaped

Mushroom Ring Type

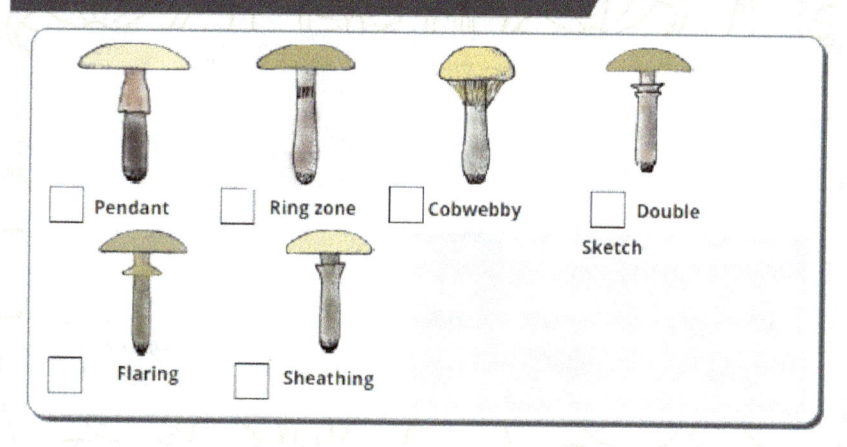

- [ ] Pendant
- [ ] Ring zone
- [ ] Cobwebby
- [ ] Double Sketch
- [ ] Flaring
- [ ] Sheathing

REFERENCES

Baldwin. S. (n.d.). Golden Currant. Santa Fe Extension Master Gardeners. https://www.sfemg.org/2020-blog/golden-currant-ribes-aureum

Chihuahua Desert Plants: Edible for Survival. (n.d.). Prezi.com. https://prezi.com/msawt3hfplhh/chihuahua-desert-plants-edible-for-survival/

Bruneni, S. (n.d.). NOVEMBER : One-seed juniper : Juniperus monosperma. Santa Fe Botanical Garden. https://santafebotanicalgarden.org/november-2011/#:~:text=The%20US%20Forest%20Service%20estimates

Dandelion: Pictures, Flowers, Leaves and Identification | Taraxacum officinale. (2019). Ediblewildfood.com. https://www.ediblewildfood.com/dandelion.aspx

Fireweed: Pictures, Flowers, Leaves and Identification | Chamerion angustifolium. (2019). Ediblewildfood.com. https://www.ediblewildfood.com/fireweed.aspx

New Mexico, Living Landscapes | New Mexico Museum of Natural History & Science. (n.d.). Www.nmnaturalhistory.org. Retrieved September 23, 2022, from https://www.nmnaturalhistory.org/online-exhibits-bioscience/new-mexico-living-landscapes

Mushroom Foraging in Taos. (n.d.). Taos.org. https://taos.org/discover/mushroom-foraging-in-taos/

Purslane: Pictures, Flowers, Leaves & Identification | Portulaca oleracea. (n.d.). Www.ediblewildfood.com. https://www.ediblewildfood.com/purslane.aspx

Signs of Spring along Bear Creek in Southwest New Mexico | Casitas de Gila Nature Blog. (2011, April 3). Casitas de Gila Nature Blog | Happenings in the Natural World of Southwest New Mexico. https://casitasdegila.com/blog/springtime-amongst-the-cottonwoods.html

September : Parry's agave : Agave parryi. (n.d.). Santa Fe Botanical Garden. https://santafebotanicalgarden.org/september-2018/

Wildflowers of New Mexico. (n.d.). Www.wildflowersnm.com. https://www.wildflowersnm.com/Wildflowers_of_New_Mexico/Amaranthus_palmeri.html

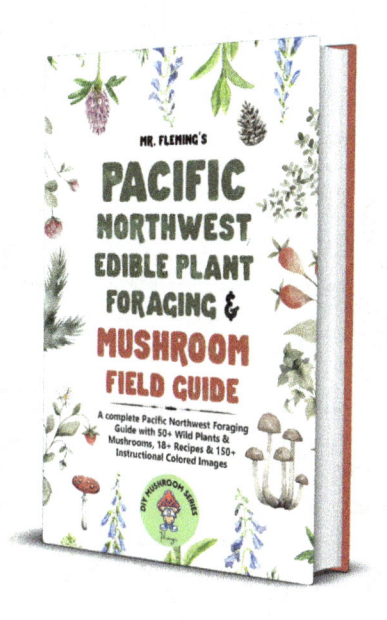

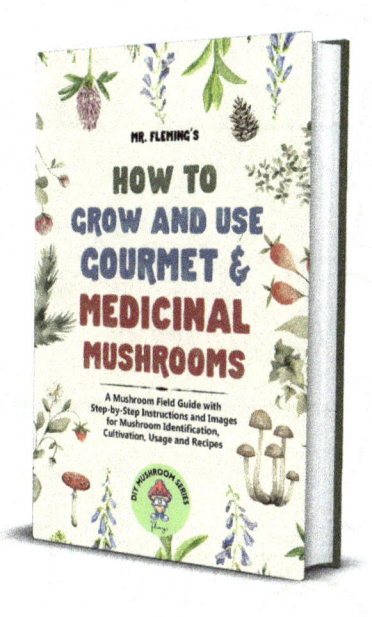

We'd Love Your Feedback!

⭐⭐⭐⭐⭐

Please let us know how we're doing by leaving us a review.

Notes

Notes

MR. FLEMING'S
PACIFIC NORTHWEST FORAGING STARTER HANDBOOK
A Beginner's Guide with a Step-by-Step Methods to Identify, Harvest, Prepare, Preserve and Cook Wild Foods
MR. FLEMING'S
MAGICAL MUSHROOM COLORING BOOK
Adult Coloring Book for Mushroom Lovers
DIY MUSHROOM SERIES
Fleming's
MR. FLEMING'S
THE MUSHROOM CULTIVATION GUIDE
A Beginner's Bible with Step-by-Step Instructions to Grow Any Magical Mushroom at Home
MR. FLEMING'S
THE MEDICINAL MUSHROOM STARTER HANDBOOK
18 Healing Mushrooms, Foraging & Usage Tips, Recipes and FAQ's

CPSIA information can be obtained
at www.ICGtesting.com
Printed in the USA
BVHW061225060123
655723BV00008B/256

9 780645 454451